LOW CEILING

LOW CEILING

A World War II Pilot's Diary

R. L. (Dix) Loesch

VANTAGE PRESS
New York

FIRST EDITION

All rights reserved, including the right of
reproduction in whole or in part in any form.

Copyright © 2002 by R. L. (Dix) Loesch

Published by Vantage Press, Inc.
516 West 34th Street, New York, New York 10001

Manufactured in the United States of America
ISBN: 0-533-14282-2

Library of Congress Catalog Card No.: 2002090738

0 9 8 7 6 5 4 3 2 1

Contents

Preface vii
USS Nassau *en route to Attu* x

Low Ceiling 1

Epilogue 47

Preface

In the spring of 1943, a singular battle between Japan and the United States was fought. Singular, because the battle was to decide possession of one of the most militarily useless, isolated, barren, storm-wracked islands in the world—Attu, the western-most island of the Aleutian Chain.

In spite of their having no military or strategic value, the Japanese did occupy the islands of Attu and Kiska as a diversion to the Battle of Midway. But as a result of their humiliating defeat at Midway, and as a sop to their feelings, they claimed a great victory in occupying the islands.

President Roosevelt and his staff, for perhaps the only time during the war, allowed their emotions to pre-empt their judgment, and with the theme of "no foreign occupation of sacred American soil," ordered the retaking of the islands.

Both sides would have been better off by completely ignoring the Aleutians.

Although tiny in proportion to the total scope of the war, the retaking involved significant resources, which could have been more effective elsewhere. Three battleships, a small aircraft carrier, and numerous supporting ships and transports were assembled to retake Attu. Nearly 600 Americans died in the effort, with the Japanese losing nearly 2,400 men.

I was a fighter pilot on board the small escort carrier assigned to the Attu force. Some naval officer with a macabre sense of humor must have picked a carrier with the name USS *Nassau* to give air support in an area of the world where the worst and most rapidly changing vicious weather occurs.

"The weather is chronically unsettled, often bursting out in violent and unpredictable tempests with the famous williwaws creating a menace to any movement of ships or planes. Rain, snow, mist, or a low, thick overcast may be expected 365 days a year in the Aleutians" (*History of United States Naval Operations in WWII*—Morrison).

On board the *Nassau,* there was one squadron of 24 pilots with 26 F4F Wildcat airplanes; 3 Marine pilots and 3 photographic F4Fs, and an SOC-3a airplane. The carrier was so short that the deck could not be seen when landing—one had to depend on the signal officer's judgment. The short deck and slow ship's speed precluded takeoffs except by catapult. Of all the aircraft carriers utilized by the United States in the war, this type was the most limited. From a pilot's viewpoint, a more unsuitable type of carrier to operate in the Bering Sea could not have been chosen. And, of course, landing in the water, unlike the South Pacific, was fatal unless picked up immediately.

Prior to the battle of Attu, my first combat action was in the taking of Guadalcanal, followed by a vicious carrier battle (the eastern Solomons) during which I shot down one Zero but my carrier (USS *Enterprise*) was severely damaged. I flew to the USS *Saratoga,* which was shortly thereafter torpedoed. Some of us were ordered to fly to Guadalcanal to help in the defense of the island. After my shooting down one more

Zero, they shot me down, with my plane riddled and a bullet wound through my leg. Through all of this, it was apparent that although our Wildcats had great durability and better firepower, our planes' aerodynamic qualities were inferior to those of the Zeros. When I had recovered from my wound and was assigned to Butch O'Hare's* squadron, now being equipped in San Diego with the new Hellcats (F6Fs), it was most wonderful to learn that we now had a fighter with qualities superior to the Zero. Imagine my feelings, along with those of a few others who had been my compatriots in battle, when we were suddenly ordered to temporary duty in a new squadron to some unknown destination, and, worst of all, flying the old Wildcats.

So I hope the brave reader of this diary will forgive a certain testiness and disgruntlement in the beginning. However, in a small group of highly trained men, facing great risks on every flight, and where maximum cooperation is essential, dissatisfaction rapidly disappears or else the individual does. Although thinly disguised as a letter, any reviewer would have immediately recognized this as a diary written in violation of wartime regulations. I can only hope that after so much time had elapsed, I will be forgiven and not court-martialed.

---

*O'Hare Airfield in Chicago is named after Butch.

USS *Nassau* en route to Attu

LOW CEILING

Low Ceiling

April 22, 1943

Dear Dad:

I'm starting this letter not with the idea of finishing it now, but rather of running it over a long period—or, at least, until I will be allowed to mail it to you. It may cover days or weeks or even months. I'll try to add to it from time to time, and that will aid me in easing my conscience about writing.

It seems as if fate has taken a perverse turn; I guess after the sweet comes the bitter or maybe it's vice versa. Anyway after the way things were going at one time in San Diego, things looked pretty good. I was working hard at something I liked and was interested in. Then the Navy and their damn fool ways have contrived to turn me into a fairly bitter lad, as of late. I wouldn't, and neither would the others, feel that way if we didn't know that there was absolutely no necessity for it.

Well, anyway, they finally did manage to get us all aboard the U.S.S. *Nassau*—a converted carrier—a squadron entirely unprepared for sea, much less actual action. For the past few days now, we've been operating in Southern California waters trying to whip our outfit into shape. I think the record speaks for itself. In the last five days we've lost from one squadron three pilots seriously injured; one pilot minorly injured; an enlisted man killed while watching carrier landings; seven airplanes almost completely wrecked, and the squadron strung all along the coast because the weather closed in at an inopportune moment. None of the accidents or crashes were occasioned by those of us who have had experience. You can't do much when every day finds you flying with a new man. Maybe I'm wrong, but I think I've always been fairly easy to satisfy; you can imagine when I say I've never been so disgusted. Cash and I, and a couple of others who came over with us, are nearly ready to say the hell with it. Maybe that's the wrong attitude when you're fighting a war to the death, but the trouble is we're not even fighting.

We have had nothing official, but we're fairly sure we're headed for Kiska and Attu in a big amphibious force in an effort to knock these Japs out for good. Of course, by the time you get this, you will have known or guessed.

Enough kicking for today.

Cash and I are rooming together. He's a mighty OK guy from Bismarck. Hope we're able to see this Aleutian thing through.

More later.

April 23, 1943

We're finally off. Yesterday finally ended with very minor casualties compared to what it looked like for a while. And unexpectedly and most opportunely, the ship put back into San Diego to pick up some more planes and equipment. By pulling every string I could,

I managed to get ashore until midnight, during which time, you can jolly well imagine, I spent with Bud and Joyce, Bea and Greg, and Cash and Ruth.* Certainly was a wonderful break to get to see Greg even if for such a short time. Golly whiz, it felt good to see him. He and Bea are a great couple and are really ideally suited. Greg will be heading for home soon, so I'll leave all his news and how he looks for you.

We made a rendezvous with the rest of our task force today. We now have our carrier, the battleship *Pennsylvania*, six destroyers, and a tanker. We're heading northwest full tilt and expect to meet many more naval forces along the way. As far as we can judge now, it all seems to have been planned very well and thoroughly. We feel fairly sure the Army is making the landing under heavy naval and air protection. Three of the BB's the Japs claimed to have sunk at Pearl Harbor are going to be with us to help blast away at them. Cash and I are guessing we'll hit them about the 4th or 5th. They won't be able to retire into the hills and jungle the way the did at Guadalcanal. If all goes as it should, I think we'll get away with fairly light casualties. We should have complete air and artillery

---

*Malcolm (Bud) Loesch was my cousin, who joined the Navy about six months after I did.

Gregory (Greg) Loesch (younger brother to Bud) and I started Naval Air Training together—he as a Marine pilot. He became one of the true heroes as a part of Joe Foss's famous squadron defending Guadalcanal. He was a holder of the Navy Cross and most unfortunately was killed in a training accident shortly after his return to the States.

Francis R. (Cash) Register was a close friend all through Advanced Carrier Training and as a member of the group of us transferred from the *Saratoga* to Guadalcanal.

control. Personally, I think our biggest enemy is going to be the weather. All reports indicate it to be fairly nasty. It seems quite likely we'll head back for the States after several days up there, but I'm not banking on it.

Nearly chow time. Cash and I have both showered and shaved. I'm reading a book of good mystery and ghost stories, and have been playing the phonograph quite a bit. Have gone through Tchaikovsky's Fourth twice today. Golly, his music is enjoyable and lasting. I guess I wrote about hearing Horowitz play his concert about four weeks ago or so. I find that music definitely satisfied something inside, and that after going a long time without hearing some, I have a real craving for it. Guess I don't need to tell you about it. Sure would have been grand if I'd had the music touch.

This letter is going to be pretty much subjective since I've lost all touch with anything in the States.

Time to chow.

April 24, 1943

Today began with a hard thump for me. I sleep in the upper bunk. When the alarm clock (which, by the way, is the one you gave me, and is one of my most prized possessions) went off, I woke out of a sound sleep and rolled out of bed to shut it off. I rolled right off for a distance of about five feet and gave myself quite a jolt. Cash heard me whack the deck and he humped like an Indian, and then fell to laughing while I slowly hoisted myself back up in my bunk. Luckily I wasn't hurt. But it didn't hurt my spirits any (as I have been in good ones all day), so it must not have been the wrong side of the bunk anyway.

We've been doing nothing but steaming north full tilt, but we got all of the major dope today. I think most of us are disappointed. Not that it isn't planned well; it just isn't what we expected and hoped for. Nothing is being done to Kiska. Our whole force consisting of 3 battleships, 1 carrier—the *Nassau*—7 destroyers, 4 troop transports, and 2 heavy cruisers, are attacking Attu alone. The attack day is now tentatively set for May 7 (another 7). Our job is going to be to provide air coverage for the whole operation, if necessary. Our outfit is composed solely of 26 F4F-4s. The Army and the Navy, operating from our nearest Aleutian base (250 miles away), have about 150 planes of all types that are supposed to support during the attack, but in the kind of weather we're expecting, I doubt if we'll see much of them. Our information is that the ceiling is rarely over eight hundred feet and that snow and icing conditions largely prevail. Nice flying weather!!

The Army is making the landing and doing all ground work. No air opposition is expected, but I think we'll meet some. In any event, it's going to be a mighty tough job. We're the only place to land within 250 miles and if we pick up a fish (torpedo), it's going to be mighty cold landing in that Bering Sea.

It seems foolish to bypass Kiska, which is 160 miles to our eastward, but they must believe the move to be worthwhile. The original plan was to take Kiska, but not enough transports were available, so here we are, headed for Attu. We expect to stay up there three or four days, giving air coverage. My bet is it will be much longer. It's very mountainous and rocky, and presents the hardest kind of beaches for landing. My guess is that we'll be lucky to have full control before two weeks are up. And then, too, it's only 1,825 miles

(I looked it up) from Tokyo and the Japs may rush some strong forces up—especially to Kiska. At the same or nearly same time we hit, I think we may stir in the South Pacific, and Greg bears me out in this. A coordinated attack will greatly help both ends.

Time for chow.

April 25, 1943

Very quiet; no flying, only standby duty. We picked up eight more ships today—four troops transports, a heavy cruiser, and three cans (destroyers). We're headed for a place called "Cold Bay," which lies almost at the tip of the Alaskan Peninsula. From there we will proceed with the rest of our force.

Today we spent a lot of time going over the general outline of the operation with intelligence officers; the details we'll work out day by day. The weather, the geography, our mission, the opposition expected, and many other things we waded through today. There are a hundred other things to know and learn before the big day. It's amazing the complexity of an amphibious operation. To see it start with a single mission and mushroom out to a definite job for each individual is an inspiring thing.

The geography and weather are going to present tremendous difficulties, not only to our ground forces, but to the planes. We'll undoubtedly run into the stiffest kind of Jap resistance. The islands are exceptionally mountainous and entirely barren so that they cannot possibly withdraw and exist.

More later.

April 26, 1943

Very dull day. The latitude and longitude increase rapidly day by day, so that a few more days will see us in Cold Bay.

The wind has been from our stern and the Task Force commander doesn't want to turn into the wind even to launch combat air patrol, so we've been doing no flying. However, we have been studying, nearly four or five hours a day, the island and all the details connected with our projected occupation. There is a sizable part of our fleet in Aleutian waters, so they are evidently expecting—or at least, being ready—for Jap counter efforts.

I was down the radar plotting room today talking to Scotty, our fighter director officer. He and the other radar officer both remembered radar school very well and when I asked if they knew my brother, they said, "Do you mean Buck Loesch?"* They claim he really knew his stuff—seemed to be an expert on the antenna end of it—and taught it well. Certainly was music to me. I don't know of any other subject that is so vitally important.

The flight surgeon and another of the boys are chewing the fat with Cash, so I'll leave off here and join the bull session.

---

*Buchanan Loesch—my brother, a radar expert at MIT, who, when he joined the Navy, was immediately assigned to instructing military personnel.

April 27, 1943

We have been doing nothing but moving steadily north. This evening we are about seven hundred miles from the coast and two hundred miles north of the U.S.-Canadian boundary. The temperature is lower, about thirty-five and a high wind is blowing. The ship is heaving and rolling, and creaking and groaning.

We haven't flown a hair since leaving San Diego, and I'm rapidly feeling worse every day. It's almost too cold to get any exercise, and one can't read and study all day, so taken as a whole, I'm not feeling too sharp tonight. However, a shower has helped a lot. . . .

Taken as a whole, we three were certainly most fortunate to get together at all, but it surely seemed tough to me to have to leave just after Greg got in after I'd been there all that time.

Cash has a bad cold and so do many of the other boys; a couple have cases of trench mouth. I'm doing my best to try not to get either, but it's mighty easy to pick up a cold when you are continually with those who have one. I need to have a tooth looked at, but I am going to try and hold out until I get back(?).

April 28, 1943

Another flyless day. We expect to hit Cold Bay day after tomorrow.

Submarine scare today. A destroyer picked one up on its detecting apparatus and dropped some depth charges. I think there was one there, although I feel sure we didn't get it. If so, I feel sure he'll be able to get a contact report off to Japan. We'll undoubtedly see some Japs ships and planes now, and possibly even a

8

carrier. I sure hope not, but I'm afraid it can't be helped. However, I think we have a sufficient force to take it anyway. The Japs number about 1,700 on Attu; we're landing about 6,000 Army men, backed up by 14-inch guns and nearly 200 planes. Of course, the weather and terrain are against us.

Chow time.

April 29, 1943

These pages are rambling on to such length that I am afraid they will be uninteresting. However, during these infernally non-busy days, I can hardly help but find myself sitting at my desk. It is, at present, littered with all the past letters that I have received in the last few days, and months. One shelf is completely crammed with secret material, which, so far, I have failed to study too well. At my right is a book, which I have nearly finished reading—an enjoyable book too. *Trelawny,* by Margaret Armstrong. Well written, about a fascinating character, and describing hectic times.

We were scheduled to fly today, so I was looking forward to fly time. Another disappointment; we're in such a hurry, they can't take time out to launch and recover us. We all got out to watch the *Pennsylvania* fire her main batteries, and that was called off at the last moment as well. Very discouraging. I'm beginning to not like our O.T.C. (Officer in Tactical Command), who is aboard the *Pennsylvania.*

Cash and I had our pictures taken in our planes a few days ago, and I've just run down and gotten the prints now. They turned out fairly well and the next chance I get—which I don't expect to be too soon—I'll send a couple on.

Cash's cold is worse and he's been spending most of his time in bed; hope I don't pick it up just in time to put me off on "dog" day. Cash and I both figure that this cruise is—in a way—our worst so far. We figure that the mission we're on may very easily not depend on skill; i.e., a fire, weather, or the williwaws can kill the best aviator, while one, at least, feels that skill and experience can count for something against other planes. Well, there's nothing to do but wait and see. We broke out our winter flight gear; it's getting devilish cold now. However, I could wish that it would get much colder, because they expect the temperature to hang right around thirty-two degrees, and that's the worst temperature for icing conditions. Again we'll just have to wait for a streak of luck.

April 30, 1943

Last day of April has been a cold crisp day. We sailed through ocean much greener than any of the Pacific I've ever seen before. Our task force and the transport group on our starboard beam plodded steadily on until late this afternoon pure white mountains rose sheer out of the water ahead of us. In places the sky was overcast, at times snowing, and breaks would show the sun and sky to be flawlessly blue and the air as crisp and invigorating as Rocky Mountain air. We moved slowly by majestic snowy peaks, among rock pinnacles, and tiny rock islands bare of everything but tawny tundra grass. The Aleutians are bare of growth except for this wild hardy grass. It will be a long lifetime ere I forget these islands. Even with their complete uninhabitable aspect, they hold a fascination for me that the South Pacific archipelago never held. Finally, just at dusk, which is very long, we moved to the very end of Cold Bay where we joined with our other forces. We now number three battleships, one carrier, either five or six transports, and sixteen destroyers. Later we will pick up strong cruiser and destroyer forces. At present we expect to lie to the bay here for two days while all last-minute plans are discussed and all the ships are topped off.

Attu is only 640 miles from the nearest Jap islands, so I expect to see some planes from Japan and probably some from Kiska. I actually believe that the Japs are being starved out of the Aleutians. For well over a month now, our blockade has been so effective that no supplies have reached them, and the 10,000 men on Kiska don't live on tundra grass—even though they be so near animal.

Time to hit the hay.

May 1, 1943

This morning turned up mighty gloomy looking, but, at least, we didn't have to get up at 5:00. The morning drifted by with most of us playing cards or checkers or listening to the radio. It looked as if the whole day would be spent just as indolently. But shortly after lunch when our hearts' game was in full swing, the executive officer of the ship came in and announced that a boat was going ashore for all the officers having specific business. We figured that let us out, but Blair asked him if we could go anyway. He said, "No, not unless you have specific reasons." Of course," he said, "I don't have to know what your business is." We rose as a body, whipped into our winter flight gear, and went ashore to get our feet on land again, to look the place over, and to guzzle a few beers. It snowed and sleeted all afternoon, and the ceiling was never over three or four hundred feet. Pretty good day, the boys claimed who are stationed here. There is a remarkably good field here and great quantities of supplies. In fact, the Army and Navy have done great work in Alaska and the Aleutians. Amazing what can be done under such adverse conditions.

Tomorrow we expect to operate in the bay and get in a little flying. Hope I won't be disappointed again.

We were allowed to send out mail today. If I was limited in my letters, as I was today, I think I could always keep up on my correspondence. I sent off a big cache of them, identical to the one I sent you, and this cleared up nearly all my letter debts.

Everyone wanted to see a show so badly that they moved the planes, or most of them, to the flight deck and while I'm writing this, I can hear the blood and thunderous noise of *Northwest Passage* echoing through the ship. I managed to sit through part of it, but gave it up. Never could see anything to it.

Pretty sleepy tonight.

May 2, 1943

Our communications officer tells us that liquor has been rationed in the States. Great hullabaloo aboard ship; much yelling and screaming. Ration meat, food, shoes, gas, rubber, and the Navy won't kick, but ration their liquor supply and you'd think their greatest necessity in life had been seriously curtailed.

All day we spent sitting in the bay while it snowed and sleeted. Flights were all canceled, as I had previously feared. "Dog" day seems to have been set later, so we don't expect to leave here for nearly two more days. We played bridge, checkers, and hearts; finally—like a bunch of giggling girls—we played a couple of hours of "Old Maid," laughing and shouting as if it were the greatest game in the world. I think some of the other officers looked askance at us, but they couldn't help but get interested; we were having too much fun.

We had operated on this ship a week before we left San Diego. I made about five hops during that time and each one of them was a catapult take-off. One more type of qualification. It's very simple and effective. You taxi onto the gear, the mechs attach the cable, you rev the motor up to take off power, put your head back against the rest, move your left arm across your chest signifying your readiness; there is a sudden stomaching lurch and there you are flying along. Very neat.

Off to the old sack.

May 3, 1943

Today was egg day, so I rose early enough to eat breakfast and proceeded to quaff down two delicious soft-boiled eggs. At lunch we had rice again for the third or fourth time; that's an ill omen, as I well know. As a rule, though, our mess aboard this ship has been excellent.

You can see how low I'm getting for news when I have to comment on the food. When we're as idle as we have been for the past two weeks, the meals constitute about the only pleasant breaks during the dull, dull days.

I seem to be picking up the standard cold at just the wrong time. I'm not sure yet and consequently am gulping down huge quantities of water, and munching apples all day. May be able to stave it off.

Starting early this morning, a fifty-five knot wind hit us and it has been howling and lashing away ever since. Our amphibious plans have been altered again, and the Army has finally decided on a entirely different way of making the landing. It looks better to me than any of the previous ideas. We expect to get under way in the morning and head full tilt west. We'll swing north of the Aleutians and come onto Attu from the north. Our chances of approaching unobserved are favorable, although I'd rather risk the chance of discovery, and trade it for better weather. I honestly don't see how we can operate under the conditions that have been prevalent around here. And besides, I expect some deck trouble after our long lay-off. Hope not.

Nothing more today.

May 4, 1943

I woke up fairly early, so I ate some breakfast, even though it wasn't an egg day. Soon the bos'n piped under way, and very shortly one could feel the motion as we put to sea. We left the harbor last and had the last view of Cold Bay. The destroyers and battleships went first. We could see the black hulk of the battleships standing out to sea eight or ten miles from us, and it was hard to believe that they contained power enough to destroy us at that range.

We are pushing through the Bering Sea now with a high gale roaring around us. We stood at flight quarters today, but I'll be darned if I know why. It was much too rough to operate off this crackerbox. Here was the weather data I put down on my chart when I came on duty at 3:00 o'clock this afternoon.

Wind—30 knots from 283
Ceiling—1,000 feet
Visibility—3 miles
Temp.—1.1 C
Dew Point 1.0 C
Bad wind squalls.

That's quite a pill to take in itself, to say nothing of trying to operate off a carrier in stuff like it.

Finished the *Greene Murder Case.*

May 5, 1943

General quarters was at 4:28 A.M. this morning, so you can see we're really getting up early.

I feel lousy today. My cold has crystallized and descended upon me with all the fury of a bad cold. Woe is me; why did it have to come now when the attack is less than three days away?

Radar picked up a bogey, and they were just on the point of launching our two divisions when it was identified as friendly. The way things have been going, I'll be mighty surprised if we ever take off from this ship.

We listen to Radio Tokyo nearly every morning. We're so much closer to Japan than to the States that all the music and radio reception, in general, is much better from Tokyo. It is also a very reassuring feeling to wake up bleary eyed, eat breakfast in a stupor, and be suddenly brought to by the casual voice of a news announcer reporting the sinking of another U.S. fleet; we must have a helluva lot of fleets; thus, the reassurance. But they play pretty good music and except for all the dirty names the announcer calls the Americans, it isn't half bad.

Recent reports indicate that the A.A. fire on Attu and Kiska is much stronger. Neither island has received any known supplies due to our heavy blockade, so I don't see how they can have too much. However, that remains to be seen. The northernmost Japanese island, Paramishiru, has a naval base and probably airfields. I'm expecting strong counter action, since it is only 640 miles from Attu.

We move steadily westward while our plans become perfected to the last details. We now have exact targets assigned to us. One thing about this war is that we've figured and carried out some of the most difficult of amphibious tasks. With many more of these operations taking place, we should build up a lot of useful experience.

May 6, 1943

This has been the most beautiful day we've seen on this cruise. The sky has been clear as possible, and the air as crisp and invigorating as a man could want. It looks as if we may get this kind of weather on the 8th, but it's hard to be sure.

My cold is worse today, but I feel better. I know I have a fever, but darned if I'll go to the doc unless it gets much worse; he might ground me.

My opinion is that the boys running our Army and Navy still don't know how to use air power. Granted that we're building enough of them and that, in general, the big boys recognize their potentialities and uses; the trouble is in their thought processes. It seems to me (I may be wrong, just because I'm on the operational end of things) that they always start thinking about an operation like this in terms of troops, ships, guns, etc., and then at the end, after they've coordinated everything else, they toss in what air power they think is necessary. The result is an amazingly complicated structure for the air power. We have to learn hundreds of different kinds of flare signals, star shots, radio authenticators, line markers, restricted areas, recognition signals and codes, and a seemingly endless stream of odds and ends. I believe if they start their thought processes with the planes, making and building all signals and transmissions round a greatly simplified coordination between the planes and all other forces, that all operations would run off much smoother and the planes would be many times as effective. It seems to me that we have still failed to learn our lesson from Crete where the Germans coordinated and simplified everything for their aircraft. Maybe I'm talking through my hat, but I'll stick to it until proven otherwise.

The way things look now, we will stay around Attu during the 8th and 9th and then accompany the transports either back to Kodiak or the States. If this goes through, my prediction is that we'll hit San Francisco about the 19th or 20th. Be interesting to see how close I come. Hope Bud is still in San Diego. I expect Greg and Bea will be at the ranch.

May 7, 1943

Final plans gone over today. We worked most of today, if sitting around studying maps, photographs, schedules, signals, and a hundred other things could be called work. You should see the thick pile of material that was issued to each pilot; I feel like a banker with a satchel full of securities.

Cash and I feel that our divisions have the toughest and most important job in the whole air end of this thing. We take off at 8:30 with eight other planes. Those eight make a dawn attack on specified targets while our eight circle the island looking for anything out of the way. Then we take up combat air patrol. We are loaded with a 100-pound demolition bomb, a 50-gallon belly tank, and 1,200 rounds of 50-caliber ammunition. Ten minutes before the boys hit the beach, the shelling will stop and during that lull in there, it's entirely up to us to drop our bombs and strafe the beach areas so that *none* of our boys will be lost before they hit the beach. I think we can do it, but it's going to be tough and require the maximum in judgment and precision. Those boys are really depending on us during those few bad minutes, and if we press home our attacks and do our job right, it will immeasurably add to their confidence once they're ashore. The A.A. fire will probably be medium, but we'll have to go so low that it's going to be mighty dangerous. Cash and I worked out what we thought was the best plan and then we had a good long bull session with our divisions. Here's hoping we have good luck.

The announcement was just made that due to weather the attack will be postponed a day.

I've forgotten to mention that I'm letting my mustache grow again; this time I'll try a more dapper type. Won't stay long with me, though.

May 8, 1943

We've done nothing but float around in the Bering Sea about two hundred miles north of Attu all day. We have weathered the worst storm I've ever seen, and it's only just now abating. We had a maximum roll of 30° today, and although that may not sound like much, I can assure you that for a ship this size, it is very near the limit. All day long the wind has raged and mountainous seas gnashed their way over the ocean. Many of the boys were plenty sick, and I bet there's a lot of blue Army boys aboard the transports. Hope not, because sea sickness will impair their ability about as much as anything.

As far as we know, and it is late afternoon, the attack comes off tomorrow. If we can just get some decent weather for only a few hours, it will be sufficient. We're keeping our fingers crossed.

Whoopee! We were listening to the radio last night and picking up all the wonderful news about Tunisia. I think that it's a good example of how quickly overwhelming air power can destroy an army's ability to fight. The war's still a long ways from ending, but we're getting there and playing the tune now.

Time to shave and shower.

May 9, 1943

Late last night big news came in. A big Jap convoy is evidently heading this way. So—we are holding off our attack, at least, until the 11th. Two cans, the five transports, and our ship are all circling about three hundred miles northeast of Attu. The battleships, cruisers, and tin cans are all west of Attu in an attempt to intercept the Japs. Two more battleships and two more tin cans are heading this way from Pearl Harbor, so they evidently expect the Japs to make a real effort. It looks like a big scrap. We are expecting to proceed into Attu if they haven't hit here by the 11th. Maybe these Aleutians will prove the Japs undoing, even though they are the most desolate places in the world. Some of our boys who were on the *Wasp* when she was in Scapa Flow say that they used to say it would serve the Germans right if they took the place. These islands are so utterly devoid of anything that it may serve us right to take them. However, we may be able to use them against Japan someday.

I'm over my cold and have felt fine the last two days. Of course, I've been so inactive that I don't think I'll ever be in shape again. Navy life at sea certainly is hard on the old constitution. I try to take good care of myself though and eat very lightly and drink a lot of water. Works quite well but I never feel as well as I do when I'm ashore. One of the things that always bothers me is sleeping in a completely closed, completely dark little room. I don't think I'll ever get used to that after the way I've been used to sleeping.

Time to chow.

May 10, 1943

My one big regret was that yesterday I wasn't able to send or say anything to Peggy. Mother's Day came and went with me only being able to think about her and not do anything about it. I guess I let your birthday slip by without saying anything either, but I'll be darned if I even know how many years you number.

It's after chow and we feel fairly sure that the attack is definitely coming off tomorrow morning. So far nothing more has been heard about the Japs but I, personally, feel sure they're a'coming. I gave my plane a final check this afternoon; seems OK. I'll give $50 if I can just have a good radio tomorrow.

Hope this letter reaches you if this happens to be the last entry. The imminent prospect of dying doesn't bother me a bit except that I'm afraid you all might worry or grieve. If that should happen, I want you to know that I hold no grudge in the world and that my only wish is that this war may soon end so that you will all know peace again. Awfully hard to put down on paper how one feels about these things, but I think you pretty well know how I feel anyway.

Well, maybe I'd better sign off.

May 12, 1943

Big day yesterday and I'm skipping a little time I should be spending in the ready room to write about it while it's still fresh in my mind.

Just found out I was out of paper, so you'll have to damn this thin paper and try to read it anyway.

We got up at 4:00 A.M., and ate a hurried breakfast. General quarters came about 5:00. They bag down all the hatches then and make the ship water tight throughout, so that one almost has to stay at his general quarters station. For the pilots it's always the ready room.

It was dark and gloomy at that time, and the fog was about as thick as any I've ever seen. The ship was just barely moving along on a sea as slick as a mirror; two destroyers ran into each other and were forced to return to Adak. Our first hop was scheduled for 5:30.

We didn't make it and all other operation plans were canceled or, at least, postponed. Finally, about 7:00 the fog lifted, leaving us a really wonderful day for this neck of the woods. The bombardment and landing was still being held off, but it was decided to launch us anyway. So off we were shot. It felt strange to get in the air again, especially with such a heavily loaded plane, but after about fifteen minutes it became natural again.

Attu lay about fifteen miles from us, rugged and white. Our mission was to circle the island and then return to combat patrol. We could see very little, since almost as soon as we reached the island, the fog was solid thick. All we could see were the mountainous parts protruding above. But we went ahead anyway, not seeing anything or drawing any fire. But our troubles were just beginning. The fog had blanketed the ship too and when we went back to try and locate the ship, we found it impossible. We knew within a very small area where it was, but we were as gone as if it had been nearly a hundred miles away. Our gas was getting low and I was already making my plans for heading back to where I thought there were some tin cans and landing in the cold, cold water. Luckily I had excellent radio contact, and without going into details as to how it happened, the ship finally got into a halfway hazily clear area; just enough so we could see it. By telling the ship which way to turn, I managed to keep her in that area until all but one were aboard. He had landed in the water previously and been picked up. I kept my division up until the very last because I was fairly sure we had more gas than the others. You can imagine how bad it was when at one time they ordered us to proceed to Amchitka, nearly 250 miles away. It was only because we didn't think we could make it that we didn't go.

We had one barrier crash, one bad landing crash, one, previously mentioned, water landing, and one crash on deck with the landing gear damaged. Otherwise we all made it back, which under the conditions, was remarkable. Ordinarily the wind over a carrier's deck should be thirty knots, but we were landing aboard yesterday with eighteen knots. Mighty tricky and dangerous. The signal officer criticized everyone's landing that he thought necessary and then proceeded to say that Loesch made the best today; a perfect landing. I knew it was a good landing, but I didn't think it was that good. That ended air operations until later when the fog lifted again and eight more planes were launched in the afternoon. Bad weather forced them to return quickly. One of them was forced to land in the water due to prop trouble. He's OK though.

Meanwhile, they had managed to land a few scout troops under cover of the fog, and with no bombardment, the scouts moved rapidly over difficult terrain and came around in back of the main Jap establishment at Holtz Bay. This was so successful that several more battalions were landed there to follow them up. Also, the main body of troops began to land at Massacre Bay under cover of the fog. The landing was successful and was being carried out late last night when it was still as light as day. But at about 11:00 P.M., the boys were meeting stiff opposition and were under heavy shell fire, at least, according to our information. Unfortunately, neither the ships nor planes could do a thing to help them. However, I believe they'll make out all right.

This morning the sea is slicker and the fog is

thicker. The aerologist says it probably won't clear before tomorrow. So here we sit.

Some heavy formation of Army planes came over yesterday and had to return to Amchitka. One Army B-24 had two generals and a colonel; they came loaded with gas and were going to stay all day. They had excellent radio communication with the *Pennsylvania* and also with us. During the long lull, one of the generals sang a risqué song to the admiral on the *Pennsy*. They had quite a little chat back and forth. Then the admiral asked him if he could sing his song. The general said no, but he'd sing it again anyway, which he did. The Japs who must have been listening in probably thought those stupid Americans, but I like to think it was good old American companionship and humor coming at a critical time. Nothing is going to help us win this war more than that ability, even though, in this case, it was a flagrant violation of the radio discipline that they themselves had set up.

As I said nothing is happening today at all as far as we're concerned; at least, so far. If anything does I'll try to put it down later. Meanwhile I'm going to get some much needed sack time.

More same date; early evening.

Today turned out to be our big day.

The troops had advanced fairly well but were definitely stopped by heavy gun fire around Holtz Bay. The main bulk at Massacre Bay worked getting their supplies and equipment ashore. It remained closed in over Massacre Bay the whole day, but over Holtz Bay it was very clear with nearly four thousand feet almost all day.

Finally at about 12:45, they launched Cash and me and our divisions to attack the targets in Holtz

Bay. We proceeded in starting over a ridge between Holtz and Chicagof Harbor when suddenly everything seemed to go off at once. All around us at very close range, A.A. guns opened up. It was heavy, accurate, and dangerous. I made a hard turn, losing my second section, and proceeded to attack the guns in Holtz Bay. From there we also were receiving very heavy gunfire. But we managed to strafe and bomb so well that when we were through there was almost no opposing fire. I think we nearly cleaned them out and reports from the Army confirmed this. The admiral gave us a "Well Done." Luckily—and it really was lucky—none of us were lost, but many of the planes were hit by A.A. bursts. Many of them hit all around me, jouncing the plane around and making it damned uncomfortable. But we pressed home our attacks to within fifty feet of the ground, and don't think those ground troops didn't appreciate it.

Later this afternoon eight more were launched. They encountered almost no A.A. and were able to wipe out several machine-gun nests, which had been holding up our troops. They sent back and said, "Excellent work; our troops are advancing due to your fine job." You can see we're getting good cooperation and working hard to help those boys out all we can.

The battleships were able to shell most of the day, and the destroyers did some fine work. It looks as if there will still be some fairly stiff fighting, but I think the hump is behind us.

There were several groups of Army planes over today, and although I don't know, I think they did yeoman duty.

About chow time the *Pennsylvania* had a torpedo fired at her, which missed, but which heralded the

Japs' arrival. We can expect more soon. I believe that two more days here should see everything under control, so perhaps we will be leaving soon. The weather prediction is bad for tomorrow, and just for that reason, I'm thinking it might be good.

We watched the BB's shell. The carrier was in very close to the island. You can't imagine the terrifying effect of those huge guns until you hear and see them.

Sorry, must go on duty again.

May 13, 1943

The submarine that shot at the Pennsylvania was located, bracketed by the cans, and depth-charged. She was hit and rose to the surface where one of the cans sank her at blank range. Have had no trouble so far today in that line and it is now about 4:30 P.M.

I'll make a rough sketch here of Attu and then you can see what has been happening better.

In general, the situation is as follows: Scout companies were landed at Red and Scarlet beaches while the main force landed at Massacre Bay. The scout troops advanced over easier ground than expected so that three or four battalions were shifted around from Massacre and landed behind the scouts. The Red beach troops met heavy fire and stiff resistance where the arrow ends. The others are now about where the arrows end as well. The Japs were completely concentrated in Holtz Bay and Chicagof Harbor, with the exception of a few controlling gun positions between Holtz and Massacre, which have been holding up our troops. The shaded section of the west arm of Holtz is where the Japs have been giving Scarlet and Red troops so much trouble. Our big trouble so far is that

we've been unable to set up any artillery though some 105-mm howitzers have been landed. In my opinion there is no better gun in the world than our 105's, and as soon as they're set up, things will go better. So far the troops have had to depend on ship fire, which is risky and hard to coordinate, especially when the ships can't even spot their own fire.

May 14, 1943

Had to stop in a big hurry yesterday as general quarters was sounded.

Eight planes were launched later yesterday. They did a fine job in Holtz Bay. The Army units said it was excellent and the squadron received special comment from the admiral.

In general the situation has changed very little since the outline I gave yesterday. Late this afternoon the boys made a concerted attack and I think have advanced considerably.

But we have suffered a very bad day.

The weather has been bad all day. The ceiling varied from a hundred to a thousand feet and the visibility was never more than two or three miles. As soon as the weather cleared, it was expected that several air attacks would be sent in. But about 12:00 noon, general quarters was sounded on the double. Both Cash's and my divisions were launched along with eight other planes with the squadron commander. When in the air, we were given two sectors, both of which turned out to be friendly; and as long as we were in the air, we were ordered to attack certain targets. Cash was to take his planes up Massacre Bay and attack target #6. The captain was to take target #33, and I was to take

#1. I only had three planes, since the fourth one had gone in the water from the catapult. Injured but OK, I guess.

When the formation reached the island, I broke off and headed into Holtz Bay, although I knew it was a tight spot from previous days. The others headed on around the island.

Imagine if you can being boxed in by rugged, snowy mountains on three sides and a ceiling of nine hundred feet. But I entered the Bay anyway. One had to turn very sharply and fight extremely rough air and try to find our targets at the same time. After two dummy circles, I located the front line markers of our own troops. We three then proceeded to make seven or eight runs until our bombs and ammunition were expended. All this time we were encountering light AA fire and feeling pretty uncomfortable about it, since we were so low and compressed into such a tight space.

Target #1 is a ridge with our troops on the east side and the Japs on the west side. Between the overcast and the top of the hill was only about a one-hundred-feet clearance. One had to bring his plane around in a hard right turn, skimming the mountains and the Jap positions, firing at the west side of the ridge as long as possible, and then scooting through the gap. One of the most dangerous things I've ever done. But the Army boys said it was just what they wanted, so I guess it was worth it. The B-24 was hovering around the entrance to Holtz Bay watching us and reported back to the ship that those crazy pilots were doing a damn fine job.

Encountering as severe winds as I did, it still wasn't as bad as the williwaws that hit Cash's division. Cash can't even explain what happened, except that his plane was violently thrown around, and that, when he had figured everything was all over for him, he ended up in a steep dive in Holtz Bay. Two of his division crashed in the mountains and were almost certainly lost. One of them I knew very slightly, but the other I knew quite well. Damned if I know how I'm going to look his wife and little kid in the eye if and when I get back.

And, further, nobody who was with him can explain it; the captain was lost in Sarana Bay.

All in all a bad, bad day. The ship's captain has asked all pilots up to his cabin at 9:00 P.M. I think he is going to pass out some good stiff drinks; we can use them after a day like this. We are now reduced to about a 13- or 14-plane squadron out of 26, and 22 pilots out of 25, 3 of those 22 being on tin cans after landing in the drink.

We learned today that it was originally intended for the *Nassau* to only stay here one day, giving fighter coverage to the ships. Instead we have stayed four days, doing the nastiest kind of flying work. This little converted job has really done all right. I think we'll stay longer, but how much longer I don't know.

Of one thing I'm sure. We can't stay much longer without the Japs taking some mighty stiff counter measures.

Makes us laugh to listen to San Francisco and Tokyo; S.F. announces the Army occupied Attu with no opposition; Tokyo says it had already been evacuated.

Mighty glad to hear of the Axis debacle in Tunisia. In general, things look better, although from my little end of it up in this cold neck of the woods, it doesn't seem that way.

Must sign off now.

Hard to say anything about losing guys like Doug; the best way I find is to never think about it.

(By the way, I notice I've gotten my pages slightly mixed, but if you get this far, follow the numbers and you'll be OK.)

May 16, 1943

Yesterday was quiet; we did nothing but sit.

*   *   *

Fifteen-minute lapse here; general emergency bell rang. Sub contact. We're high-tailing it now, but have secured from general quarters. I think I made it from my room here up to ready room in about ten seconds. Seemed that way.

Today has been a terribly tragic one for me. Cash was killed.

The ship lay forty miles north of Attu. Under bad visibility, with the ceiling about eight-hundred feet and with icing conditions, we were rotating, strafing and bombing attacks in Holtz Bay.

The ceiling was lower than ever before and the places to strafe harder to get at.

Cash was leading the division. I was his section leader since the shuffling around after losing the three boys on the 14th. We arrived at the Bay, entered it, and began our perilous job.

I kept going around and around at full speed, dodging the A.A. (which was very accurate in such a restricted area) as best I could and picking out what targets I could. After I'd dropped both bombs and shot all my ammunition, I headed for the rendezvous point.

Cash's wingman and my wingman showed up, but after waiting nearly twenty minutes, I gave it up and went back to the ship.

We thought for a while that he might have bailed out and be in his rubber boat somewhere, but early this afternoon a dispatch from the Army saying they had found the plane and pilot confirmed the worst. We don't know anything except that he evidently was in that damned fog when he crashed into the mountains.

I guess I don't need to tell you that we've been mighty close to each other all the way so far, and a piece of me has definitely gone with him. He was one of the best pilots you'll ever see and was one of the best liked guys I've ever known. He was married to one of the finest girls I've known, and coming after Doug, I feel as if I almost can't go back to San Diego and face it. Quite frankly, I feel like getting just as stewed as I can. I'll have to start inventory on Cash's things tonight.

On the same flight with us, a Marine observation pilot took off. For some unexplained reason, his plane dived steeply into the water only two or three miles from the ship. Didn't know him at all, but it takes another of our planes and pilots. The way I look at it, though, a guy cannot keep on taking the extreme risks we're taking up here without sooner or later getting his. Every day we've flown here has been in weather that normally would be labeled the worst kind of non-flying weather. Add to it the difficulty of our mission and the answer is apparent. Without going into detail, I was extremely lucky to pull through today. At one time, I thought—

But I guess the big thing is that we're doing our job, and doing it right, because the boys on the ground say it really helps and is most effective.

Reports have it that we are going into Adak tonight. Sounds to me as if we're just going to be held in reserve up here. Same old story.

Good night.

It's going to be terribly lonely in Cash's and my room tonight.

At least, I can always talk to God.

May 17, 1943

Today marks an even month at sea for us. I was ashore in San Diego for about six hours one evening and at Cold Bay one afternoon for a couple of hours, but other than that I've seen an awful lot of ocean.

And today that ocean is as calm as calm can be. Very little danger of subs today if a good lookout is kept. I think they figure that, at least, seven or eight torpedoes have been fired at our ships, but so far none of them have registered. It's an ideal day for refueling the cans, so we're moving along at about twelve knots, approximately seventy miles north of Attu. We started to head for Adak last night, which is where Comnorpac (Command Northern Pacific) hangs out. But for some reason or other, we turned back again and we are now the only ships in Attu waters. The transports finished unloading yesterday. They are apparently bringing up more troops from Adak where they have been held in reserve for a long time.

Attu is one of five islands comprising a group called the Near Islands. Of these Attu and Agattu are nearly the same size; the other three are called the Semichis. The Semichi island lying farthest to the east is called Shenya. It is about forty miles east of Attu and about two hundred miles from Amchitka. Kiska lies almost between but only about seventy miles from Amchitka. Anyway, the Army doesn't think Attu is too feasible for an airfield and Shenya seems to be very suitable. It is entirely uninhabited, and they intend to move in there as soon as Attu is secured. The general strategy seems to be that by maintaining our present naval force, and continually strengthening the air power, we can literally starve the Japs off Kiska. It's a good idea, and I think is very possible. The only possible food they can get up here is fish, and for ten or twelve thousand men to subsist on fish would require them to turn into sea otters. If we can make our air and sea blockade tight enough, we can draw the noose, but they'll hang themselves. Or else, they'll try their hardest to get supplies through and we can make that unbearably costly.

So I figure that we will be sticking around, dodging torpedoes and such, until one either picks us off or the Army takes over at Shenya as well.

I am enclosing a dispatch from the admiral and signed by Captain Doyle. Nothing more to it than just a couple of buck-up words, but they help.

Dick Trimble and I finished the inventory of Cash's things. His desk is all shut up now and his clothes all packed. I'm only now beginning to realize his loss. May move in with a guy named Oscar Chenoweth, who is also alone since Doug's death.

Time to shave and shower for chow.

May 18, 1943

Good news.

The Army forces from Massacre Bay, and those working through Holtz Bay have met, and the remaining Japs are now completely pocketed in Chicagof Harbor. They may put up a last-ditch stand, but it should be in the bag now in, at least, another week. They seem to have done well and have managed to suffer very light casualties. So far the Army reports about 85 killed, 450 wounded, and about 70 missing. Considering that we probably have nearly 12,000 men on Attu, now those are very light casualties. I only wish our squadron had suffered in the same proportion, but, on the other hand, I think our flying attacks did as much to prevent many more Army casualties than anything else. So perhaps it has been worth the high cost we've paid.

We're still floating around way up here in the Bering Sea, refueling the cans. We should finish today.

It seems to me as if somewhere previously in this letter I estimated we might be back by the 20th if all went well. But now I'm sure we won't be back for, at least, two more weeks and probably much longer, and it's beginning to look as if we might be stationed up here.

My new mustache is much better than the other one, but it still is pretty bad. Dave Senft—an old Jax classmate—and Dick Trimble just came in, so I'll stop here.

Finished the above about 1:00 P.M. It is now 7:00 P.M. after chow.

Nothing more happened today. I've been playing Russian Banque with Foster Blair most of the afternoon. Pretty good game for two people. I've looked through the few books that are available to us time and time again and have read the few that were of interest. I was finally reduced today to drawing out *Alder Gulch* by Ernest Haycox as a means of time spending.

About this time everybody is good and sick of a cruise. After about two more weeks, one gets so used to it that it seems as if it will always go on this way.

I notice that this paper is different from the rest and much thinner, so I'll not write on the reverse side any more, especially since I have just procured a new batch from Ship's Service.

I'd like to have flown in Holtz Bay today just to see what it would look like when there weren't a lot of guns firing at you and AA bursts all around. Also, wish they would let us fly, at least, one hop every day. It would break the monotony and give us something to look forward to.

Reports indicate that there are still many submarines around, but so far we have remained miraculously (can't spell it) untouched. More tomorrow.

May 19, 1943

Well, I guess the admiral was getting a bit nervous, so he and his battleship left us this morning to head back to the States. Now, we have three cans with us and we're the only ships in Attu waters. It's a great puzzle to us all just why, but I guess there must be some reason.

For a while it looked as if it might clear enough over Chicagof Harbor to allow us to go in and strafe, so four planes were launched. It was impossible to do anything, so they returned. No accidents.

We hear from the Army that one of their big difficulties is the large number of boys who have frozen feet. It seems to me that proper foot gear would have been the first thing to have right. Anyway a B-24 came up from Amchitka yesterday and dropped eight thousand pairs of socks.

Nothing much more to say. Everybody has reached the point where card games, and what few other amusements there are, have become extremely boring. When we're not on duty, we're almost always sleeping, which seems like an awful waste of time. But these long sea cruises can take the pep out of a guy in an awful hurry.

Nothing more so I'll get a little sack time before dinner.

No sooner got into my sack than flight quarters was sounded. Two flights were launched, but both were unable to get into Chicagof, so they gave it up. My division was just getting ready to go when it was all called off again. Oh, well, we get the next hop anyway.

No accidents today except minor ones. Dick Trimble's hook skipped up the deck, just missing the 5, 6, 7, and 8 wires and finally catching the 9th. He went into the barrier but didn't go over, and about all he damaged was the prop.

We refueled a tin can this afternoon. While the hoses were strung between ships, the boys on the carrier pitched cups of ice cream and cookies, and loaves of bread to the can boys. You should have seen them crowding the rails and yelling for more. Anything like ice cream is a great luxury to a can man, as they stay at sea for long long periods of time.

Haven't heard much from the Army today, but I think they're pushing slowly into Chicagof, setting up batteries and mortars for the final push. They're taking their time and making a good job of it, using their guns and howitzers instead of men, which is as it should be. But it probably works to our disadvantage since I doubt if we'll leave now before everything is completely under control.

If only Cash were here—

Commencing today we're getting what the States are; viz. rationing. According to the Mess Manager, we have three weeks supply of food left if we ration all food to about 75 percent and everybody goes on to the same diet. Of course, for the last number of days, we have had no kind of fresh food, and lately we've been getting a lot of beans and my old friend—rice. They're breaking out the Spam, too. Oh well, I eat so little these days that it doesn't matter much what it is.

I have just eaten lunch after coming off duty. They are planning on launching a couple of flights this afternoon if the weather breaks. Unless it really clears off—and that seems to be an impossibility up here—I doubt if we can do any good in such a small space as Chicagof. Anyway, Rooney's division and mine are all set to go. Here's hoping we get a break in the weather.

Heard the engines turning up on the flight deck and thought it might be Rooney's division taking off, but they were just warming the engines. Today looks worse, if anything, to me, but if they send us off, we can give it a whirl anyway. Just about anything would be welcome relief from this ennui.

From now on this letter, or log, will probably peter out, since sleeping, eating, reading, and card playing in continuous cycles does not make for inspirational writing. The phonograph has been on the blink and all the radios are being used for communication channels, so music is also a present non-entity.

Read excerpts from Churchill's address to Congress this morning. Sounds as if the Axis lost much more than I had imagined. Of course, I suppose his figures included everything from the beginning of the war. These recent raids in Germany must be raising the very devil with the Germans and Italians. I think when the end comes we'll find that the damage—perhaps it won't have been just material damage—was much greater than estimated. This summer might very easily see the knockout punch. I can hardly imagine what it will be like to get back into civilian life again. It seems as if I've hardly ever known my life, but this war life. We were bulling just last night on how wonderful it will be to get back into civvies.

Enough reminiscing—guess I'll get a little sack time—only thing I can think of that may cause them to launch me.

It's now 11:00 P.M. I've just come from Dick Trimble's and Foster Blair's room where they, Dave Senft, and I finished off a few ounces of brandy, which the doctor issued to the pilots.

I was right; getting into my sack did cause the weather to break. Anyway Rooney's division was finally launched. They were unable to do any good, as Chicagof was closed in, although Holtz was wide open. Later in the afternoon, Chicagof was reported open, so I took my division over to take a crack at it. Looked pretty nasty. Flew at three hundred feet under heavy overcast all the way to the island.

Just at Holtz Bay, there was a clear space big enough to climb through. We got up to five thousand feet and were assigned our targets by radio from Army officers on the ground. First two runs I didn't see what they wanted us to hit, so I got up above Chicagof and nosed over. Came barreling through the overcast about three hundred knots, not knowing whether I was going to hit a mountain or the Harbor. Luckily, I came out in the clear, and we found ourselves right on the targets in the middle of Chicagof. My boys followed me, showing what a damn fool things guys will do if there's only someone ahead of them.

After a couple of more runs like that, I got the target picked out that they wanted us to hit. It was right out in the open and up high on a commanding ridge. We really worked that place over. Three more hops went over and worked over the same identical targets. I think we just about knocked them out completely so that now I think we control the passes that overlook Chicagof. Very light and inaccurate A.A. fire today. No accidents (pure luck, I think), except very minor deck occurrences.

But tonight the ship is no longer hanging in the lee of the island, and she is rolling and pitching more than at any time for the past ten or twelve days. We're heading for Adak tonight and expect to arrive late tomorrow.

Where or when or what we do from there is anybody's guess. I'll let you guess too and hit the old sack.

May 21, 1943

It's now 1:30 P.M. I've just finished the last item in Cash's inventory. Had to wait for the laundry.

There seems to be fairly accurate scuttlebutt going around that we're headed for the States after spending tomorrow in Adak. That's mighty sweet music. It's unbelievable how getting away from the States makes one appreciate our country more and more.

Well, if I can't spend my twenty-fifth birthday in the States, at least, it looks as if I'll spend it on the way there.

But well I know, that the most boring and tiresome days are the homeward journey days. They seem endless; the ship doesn't seem to progress; and there's absolutely nothing to do, except contemplating what one will do on his arrival.

Our little experiment has turned out to be quite a cruise, though it has been a mighty sad one for me.

We have no idea what will happen to us when we arrive in the States, but I expect to have the outfit split up. I'm almost sure of one thing—Trimble, Blair, Rooney, and myself will not go back to VF-3. Hope to thunder Bud hasn't left, though. Surely do want to see him again before he shoves off.

No more to write, so I'll leave you just one guess as to what I'm going to do next.

Woke up violently at 3:00 P.M. as my alarm went off, and remained on duty until 6:00 P.M. All I accomplished in that time was gaining the gin rummy championship from Blair. Very dull, very dull.

I've just finished chow and have been topside to see if there's anything to see. A small island near Adak can be seen on our starboard beam. We're only about thirty-five miles from Adak now and will probably drop anchor about ten o'clock tonight.

We received good word from Comnorpak and Comcinpac today for our participation, and special note from the Army for our raids yesterday. Reports today indicate our troops to be pushing into Chicagof Harbor and once they've cleaned that up, it will be the end of Attu and probably all of the Japanese strength in the Aleutians. Kiska is now completely surrounded by strong Naval forces—submarines and surface ships—and strong Army Air Forces operating from several different points against them. Will be interesting to see what the Japs try to do to save the large forces that they have on Kiska.

I haven't had a haircut for nearly six weeks now, so you can imagine how shaggy I am. It's nearly impossible to get into the Ship's Barber Shop since about five hundred other guys have the same idea.

No more today.

Whooopee!!! The captain just announced over the speaker system that we're headed for San Diego.

May 22, 1943

A high storm is raging away. It's about half an hour before chow, and I've just come down after a breath of fresh air. The bulkheads and beams are creaking and groaning, and the ship has a heavy lurching motion.

We rendezvoused with the *Pennsylvania,* two empty transports, and five tin cans. We kept going last night, not putting into Adak at all.

Right now we're all headed for Puget Sound where we expect to drop off the other ships and continue on to San Diego.

No more today, I guess.

May 23, 1943

Managed to crawl out of my sack for G.Q., eat a few beans for breakfast, and then crawled back into the old sack until 10:30 A.M. Then Dick Trimble and I went up to radar pilots and chewed the fat with them awhile. Twelve twin-engine Mitsubishis came to Attu from Paramushiru and hunted all over for us, not even bothering to attack the battleships. Finally they all dropped their torpedoes at a tin can and not a one of them hit. I'd like to have taken a crack at them, but they might have easily put a fish in the old *Nassau*.

The storm has abated somewhat, but the ship is still creaking and rolling. We headed straight for Puget Sound; don't know when we'll hit there.

Dave Senft and I played bridge with a couple of other guys this afternoon, and this evening the whole ship is eagerly looking forward to seeing a movie. They're showing *Charley's Aunt,* with Jack Benny, and as I remember, it was a lot of fun. Anything—even a class F movie—would be a wonderful break.

Nothing more.

Not a darn thing to say. The trip goes tediously on and our tack slowly approaches the western coast.

Too much sleep is making me feel awfully dopey.

Almost time for movie tonight.

The movie was enjoyable and certainly helped to while away a couple of weary hours. We sat around chewing the fat for a while and then moved to the wardroom where we proceeded to open a nickel crap game. I managed to lose about fifty cents.

It's about 12:00 now and before I hit the old sack, guess I'll shave and shower.

These are the kind of days which are so hard to spend. Part of life in the Navy, I guess.

May 25, 1943

Time passes so wretchedly slow! We sleep and eat; sleep and eat. Nothing more.

May 26, 1943

Today marks my twenty-fifth year, but I don't feel a year older. In fact, I feel younger since it finally warmed up enough (though still quite cold) so that we were able to lower the #2 elevator and play several good games of volley ball. The elevator is just a whiz too small, but we worked up quite a good bit of exercise. So that tonight—it's about 11:00—I feel quite spry.

Sort of a lonely birthday, though.

We expect to hit San Diego next Monday, the 31st, that's five more long days to pass away. However, I have my routine down fairly cold now. Usually get to bed about midnight after the movie and a little bridge. Have to get up for G.Q. about 4:30 A.M., eat breakfast, about 5:30 A.M., and then hit the sack until about 10:30 or 11:00. I then manage to struggle topside and take a look around at the weather and ocean; then drop into the radio shack for any late news. Eat at noon and then hit the sack again until about 4:00 P.M. or so maybe reading a bit. Neither the lights or the books are good enough to read very much. After dinner the cycle repeats.

The captain of the ship wants each member of the squadron to write to the parents of those men lost. Personally, I don't like the idea since I think that words from complete strangers are meaningless and maybe worse than nothing. But anyway I managed to write four very short notes today. Not going to write to Cash's people until I've seen Ruth.

The squadron wants me to tell her when we hit San Diego. I honestly don't see how I'm going to do it, but guess it would be the best way since no one else was anywhere near as close to them. Anyway, I'm certainly going to take Dick Trimble along with me. He is one really top guy with down (right) good common sense and tact. Comes from a farm in Illinois, which is near a little town named Trimble after his great-grandfather.

We're almost sure we'll fly ashore while the ship is still about a day out, so we may get in on Sunday.

Nothing more.

May 27, 1943

Here I am running out of paper again. Certainly have a slug of extra envelopes hanging around.

Just finished shaving and trimming my mustache. Guess it looks a mite better than the last one, but not much.

Same old routine today. The big news is that we dropped the *Pennsylvania* today and are now heading almost due south. We're only about a hundred miles off the coast. Looked good to see a friendly search plane pick us up about noon.

Blue skies today and nice mild weather, although still fairly chilly. Had our squadron picture taken today, and if it is finished before I send this, I'll enclose one along with a picture of VF-5 taken on Guadalcanal after I was hit. Blair is the only one still with me who was in VF-5, and Cash was the last one I went through ACTG with.

Stinking movie tonight.

Time for the old sack.

May 28, 1943

Having run out of movies they are going through them again, so once more tonight Roger's Rangers will scream, and plod, and push their useless way through the film version of *Northwest Passage*. It's too much for me. I'd rather sit and twiddle my thumbs.

It's getting steadily warmer. We're getting nearer to San Francisco where we'll drop the two transports.

The word is going around—and it seems to be fairly well corroborated—that we'll fly into San Diego late Sunday. The carrier won't get in until Monday, so if you're home Sunday night, you'll probably get a phone call from your wandering son.

Nothing more.

May 29, 1943

Last entry probably.

We fly into San Diego tomorrow. Everyone turned up and checked their planes today. We're getting packed tonight. Hope I'm able to get this mass of junk off to you. Imagine much of it will be fairly tedious.

Nothing more. Got to wind up things aboard.

Some of the stuff in this letter is pretty informative and some of it is really confidential. So use your own judgment about sending it around.

Not able to send VF-5 picture. Try to do so later.

Epilogue

For the first time in the Pacific, close air support was utilized to support troop landings. All such support was supplied by planes from the USS *Nassau*. For such a first, a more difficult set of circumstances can hardly be imagined—operations from a jeep carrier in the Bering Sea, in frigid wild weather, on a snow-capped mountainous island, under almost perpetually low ceilings and visibility, and (especially judged by later air-supported landings) utilizing the crudest methods of communication between ground and air.

With all these serious limitations, it is doubtful that the air support was very effective, and probably missed targets as often as hitting them, in some cases probably firing on our own troops.

But we all thought we were doing a good job—and I think, at times, it was the only thing that kept us flying and trying. All our flights were hazardous—and more than once, it seemed as if "Someone" else also had his hands on the controls.

I rejoined Butch O'Hare's squadron after returning from the Aleutians, and I made many more combat flights in operations in the Central and South Pacific. On one flight near Howland Island, I shot down a big four-engined Japanese seaplane with a large crew aboard. The Japanese had no chance against an agile, heavily armed fighter. It was like Al Capone's St. Valentine's Day massacre and continues to haunt me to this day. Sherman was right; "War is hell."

The last year and a half of the war, I was assigned to the Fighter Design Office, Bureau of Aeronautics, Navy Department, Washington, D.C.